THE SELF-AW… IGHWAY

Reflections Journal

Dr Nia D. Thomas

A Knowing Self Knowing Others Book

ISBN 978-1-7384967-3-0

Graphic Designer: Liam Beattie

Contents

Welcome, Traveller!

"The power of reflection lies in its ability to
turn experience into insight."
John C. Maxwell

The journey of self-aware leadership is an enduring one: it has no beginning and no end, other than it starts with you and ends with you.

Developing self-aware leadership is a lifelong journey of…

- reflecting on your hard skills and relational skills
- recognising your impact on others
- making decisions about how you can change and regulate your behaviour.

The intention is to create kinder, more respectful and creative working relationships. Your goal is to make other people's work lives the best they can be, taking into account your locus of control.

This journal will give you the opportunity to pause and reflect, stop and recognise, and contemplate and regulate your behaviour, using the nine CHARTABLE directions of the Self-Awareness Compass.

You may want to start your self-awareness journey by reading ***The Self-Awareness Superhighway: Charting Your Leadership Journey.*** This journal forms an accompaniment to that book. *The Self-Awareness Superhighway* will tell you all about self-awareness, self-aware leadership and the nine self-aware leadership compass points in much more detail than we'll cover here in this journal.

You can buy *The Self-Awareness Superhighway* at www.ksko.co.uk.

What Is Self-Aware Leadership?

We have been trying to get to know ourselves for centuries! The concept of self-awareness, captured in the phrase 'Know thyself', has deep historical roots associated with ancient Greek philosophers like Aristotle and Socrates.

For us, in this journal, self-aware leadership has three parts…

Layers of self-awareness	Defining the layers
Reflection of skills	An ability to recognise the self's hard skills and relational skills (our changing thoughts, feelings, beliefs, values, strengths and abilities) through reflection and introspection.
Recognition of impact	An ability to recognise how the self's hard skills and relational skills are received by, perceived by and impact others.
Regulation of behaviour	An ability to read and understand the emotions and intentions of others and respond and act wisely in social exchanges by regulating the self's hard skills and relational skills.

Your Journey on the Superhighway

Life is a complex journey of twist, turns, peaks, unexpected vistas and sharp chicanes calling for tricky manoeuvring. Most of the time, you have your head down, busily going about your day-to-day life, getting all your chores done and ticking things off your to-do list. You work hard and diligently, achieving your goals and progressing in your career. Now though, it's time for something different – something more. Something to elevate your leadership beyond good to excellent. And achieving excellence means becoming a self-aware leader.

To become a self-aware leader, you will reflect on your hard and relational skills, recognise your impact and regulate your behaviour.

To reflect on your skills, recognise your impact and regulate your behaviour, you need to create time and space to raise your perspective to a higher vantage point. You have to go from travelling on the usual major and minor roads to journeying on a superhighway. But not just any old superhighway. This will be your very own superhighway.

A superhighway is a multi-laned road where vehicles travel at high speed over long distances. As you work through this journal you might imagine a sky-road, raised above the trees, with a helicopter view of life below – a vantage point down to the river and the village, with the city skyline in the background.

You might imagine a superhighway as an under-the-sea travelator that allows you to glide along the ocean floor, or a woodland highway that takes you from treehouse to treehouse, through the forests of the world, or a Formula 1 track with the roar of fellow drivers hurtling past. Whatever superhighway you imagine, it will provide you with an objective outlook over your daily hustle from which you can achieve the reflection, recognition and regulation you need to go from good leadership to excellent leadership.

What Are Hard Skills and Relational Skills?

Think of hard skills as teachable, practical, technical skills, like fixing a bicycle puncture or typing code into a computer.

Relational skills are the non-technical thinking things, like emotions, attitudes, beliefs and biases. They're the things that are not so easy to teach or learn. You'll have probably heard them called soft skills, but in this journal we'll call them relational skills, because they really are the most difficult to develop and hone.

Consider the phrase 'It's not what you do, it's the way that you do it.' Hard skills are what you do and relational skills are the way you do it. Together, they create a yin–yang balance of what and how.

The Self-Awareness Compass

This journal provides you with nine compass points to help guide your journey along your Self-Awareness Superhighway. They will help you chart your leadership development map and plot the directions you need to travel in.

The nine CHARTABLE compass points of self-aware leadership are:

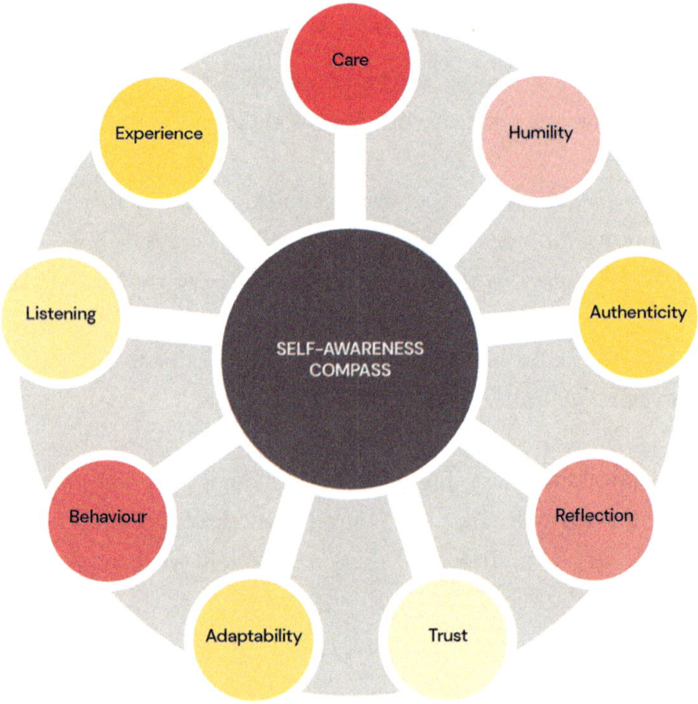

"Reflection is the teacher of wisdom."
Confucius

1. Care

If you take the superhighway of CARE, you are heading on a journey of empathy and respect, appreciating the human aspects of the lives of your colleagues whilst not shying away from having difficult conversations.

In the world of work, care is essential for the wellbeing of both individuals and the collective team. It involves navigating kindness, respect and empathy: critical waypoints for any leader. Care within the context of leadership is not warm and fuzzy; it demands honesty and the courage to engage in uncomfortable conversations. It's the acknowledgement that organisational success hinges on reciprocal care for both the organisation's vision and mission and the people contributing to achieving both. Care is the authentic, respectful and empathetic foundation of leadership.

2. Humility

If you take the superhighway of HUMILITY, your sojourn will be filled with letting others' light shine, supporting them to step forward and being open when you don't know the answers.

To be humble, you need to stay teachable, regardless of how much you already know and have already experienced. Leadership is not about being the boss, boasting or self-aggrandisement. It's an internal strength that allows you to create and foster an environment where others can shine. Humble leaders elevate their teams, recognise strengths and weaknesses and encourage growth. Humility is an acknowledgement of fallibility and mistakes, coupled with a genuine openness to learn and improve. Humility isn't a buzzword; it's integral to creating a supportive environment where mistakes are admitted, people are acknowledged and appreciated, problems are solved collectively and continuous learning is embraced.

3. Authenticity

If you take the superhighway of AUTHENTICITY, your hike will show you how to live your values, beliefs and priorities with integrity and make conscious decisions about who the professional 'you' really is.

Authenticity is a journey of self-discovery, understanding your thoughts, opinions and values. Lance Secretan describes it as aligning your head, mouth, heart and feet – thinking, saying, feeling and doing the same thing consistently. Authentic leadership demands an intimate knowledge of the many sides of who you are and a commitment to expressing your true self. It's not wearing your Saturday night sequined jacket to the office on a Monday morning nor practising your Thursday night comedy routine in the canteen on a Tuesday. It's appropriate and far more fundamental. It's about being transparent, anchored in your deep sense of self and fostering trust through openness and consistency. Authenticity in leadership is the pathway to building meaningful relationships, contributing to a healthy organisational climate and ensuring that your actions resonate with your values.

4. Reflection

If you take the superhighway of REFLECTION,
your cruise will involve being reflective in the moment
and giving yourself the opportunity to respond
rather than react, so you can grow and become
the best version of yourself.

Reflection is the beating heart of self-aware leadership, ingrained in the three-layer model of self-awareness described. It's a way to delve into the intricacies of the self, by putting up a mirror where you can examine every pore and blemish, peering into your behaviour with 360-degree vision. Steven Bartlett says, "Creativity is born in silence, mental clarity and solitude," highlighting the connection between reflection and transparency of thought. The challenge lies in finding the time and developing the habit, which this journal can help you foster. Wherever you work, reflective practice is a good habit to develop, providing a crucial pause for introspection.

5. Trust

If you take the superhighway of TRUST,
you'll trek into the land of kindness and consistency,
where you will instil trust in your colleagues
so that they choose to follow you.

Trust is not a checkbox or a proclamation; it's the essence of leadership woven into every action and decision you make. You can't simply claim trust. It's a judgement made by those around you. Self-aware leaders cultivate trust through authenticity, consistency and advocacy. Trust is a shared language of promises kept, openness in challenges and mutual respect. Building trust requires more than just words; it demands living the principles of integrity, humility and accountability underpinned by consistency of emotional response. It's the silent understanding that grows over time, yet has the potential to be obliterated in an instant. A breach of leadership trust ripples way beyond the people who you work with day to day. In its absence, relationships crumble, making way for doubt and uncertainly, eventually affecting your entire organisation.

6. Adaptability

If you take the superhighway of ADAPTABILITY, your expedition will mean responding with openness, flexibility and a growth mindset to the changing demands of your role and the changing needs of your people.

Adaptability in leadership is the art of flexing and flowing, much like a skilled pilot adjusting to different weather conditions. It's not about rigidly following plans, but rather a nimble response to change. Adaptable leaders embrace the unpredictable, adjusting their strategies like a compass finding north. It's about being open to new ideas, swiftly navigating challenges and being resilient in the face of uncertainty. Adaptability is a dynamic response to change, where leaders pivot, evolve and innovate. It's the ability to surf the waves of transformation without losing balance, steering the ship through turbulent waters with a steady hand. Adaptable leaders don't fear the unknown; they embrace it.

7. Behaviour

If you take the superhighway of BEHAVIOUR, your ride will mean modelling the behaviour you expect to see in your organisation and rewarding the behaviour of those who live the values you espouse.

Behaviour modelling is a powerful force in shaping organisational culture, as highlighted by Todd Whitaker's quote: "The culture of an organization is shaped by the worst behaviour the leader is willing to tolerate." In the context of self-aware leadership, deliberate behaviour is key – acting with awareness, choice and anticipation of consequences. A self-aware leader's every action is observed. Colleagues emulate leaders' behaviour and it creates a framework of acceptability. Poor behaviour, if tolerated and left unchecked, becomes embedded in the organisational culture, influencing the behaviour of others. Effective leaders recognise that behaviour is the primary driver of organisational culture. Ultimately, a leader's behaviour sets the standard that determines the rise or fall of an organisation's collective standards.

8. Listening

If you take the superhighway of LISTENING, you are heading on a voyage of giving voice to the quieter and marginalised people in your organisations to ensure everyone is heard.

Listening in leadership is more than just a passive act; it's the cornerstone of building meaningful connections. As Jimi Hendrix wisely said, "Knowledge speaks, but wisdom listens." It's about tuning in not just to words but also to unspoken communication, creating an environment where every voice is heard, valued and understood. In the bustling world of leadership, where voices can easily get lost, active listening becomes a vital function. Recognising the need for a listening culture, you must actively set ground rules, especially in virtual spaces, ensuring everyone gets an opportunity to contribute. Leaders must navigate the delicate balance between providing solutions and allowing voices to be heard, even if the path to understanding takes time. Listening is a daily commitment to creating a space where every voice resonates, contributing to the unity of a well-led team and a successful organisation.

9. Experience

If you take the superhighway of EXPERIENCE, your flight will mean learning from your experiences and sharing what you know with others to nurture their growth and development.

As Nelson Mandela said, "I never lose. I either win or learn." Experiential learning is at the heart of every self-aware leader's forward journey. Leadership skills evolve through cultivating, nurturing and developing abilities through experience. Learning is crucial for growth, improvement and high-level performance. Lived experience moulds leadership styles, especially when leaders have had to navigate through crises like Covid. Learning is generated by both indirect experiences, shared through mentoring and training, and direct experiences, acquired through shadowing, internships or new roles. The sharing of experiences through storytelling is vital for learning and nurturing others to grow into leadership roles. Self-aware leaders should absorb every drop of learning from their experiences and create a culture of sharing with others, to foster individual and organisational growth and resilience around them.

How to Use This Journal

"The true purpose of reflection is to transform our minds, enabling us to become architects of our own destiny."
David O. McKay

Every day, week, month or when it works for you, score your behaviour against each of the nine CHARTABLE compass directions. To do that, this journal provides you with the following phrases…

- I am caring.
- I am humble.
- I am authentic.
- I am reflective.
- I am trustworthy.
- I am adaptable.
- I model the behaviour I want to see.
- I listen.
- I learn from and share my experience.

Let's take 'I am caring' as an example.

Today, you had a team member tell you that his mother has been taken ill unexpectedly and she lives two hours' drive away. He was concerned he wouldn't be able to finish his proposal paper by 5pm. You said he shouldn't worry. You would pick up the proposal paper and work with colleagues to get it done. You recommended he spend 30 minutes with you before he left, to brief you on the progress of the paper. You also asked if there was anything else you could do.

On a scale of 1 to 9, how closely does your behaviour/actions align with the statement 'I am caring'? 1 is the most negative score, 9 is the most positive score and 5 is the neutral point. For example:

You decide to give yourself a score of 8 out of 9 because, on reflection, making him stay around for 30 minutes was not good for him and not productive for you.

Do this for all nine points on the compass.

Now, draw a line to join your nine dots together on your compass. This will give you a 'map' of where to travel on your self-awareness superhighway.

Next, note down your thoughts and words. Reflect on your hard and relational skills, recognising your impact on others and considering how you intend to regulate and change your behaviour next time. For example:

You decide that next time something like this happens in the personal life of a team member, you will recommend they leave work immediately rather than making them stay with you for 30 minutes, when their concentration is sorely lacking and they are very anxious. You're a new manager and you've never experienced this before, and you've learnt from your experience.

At the end of every reflection, you will be able to clearly see which behaviours you need to concentrate on and develop further. Below is an example of how your completed map might look. The lines on your map show you the behaviour(s) you should focus your learning and development on.

In this example, you have scored modelling behaviour and humility a 9, which means you feel confident about both. Listening is a behaviour that needs greater focus. Consider what actions you can take to regulate your behaviour to improve your listening. You might want to do this by reading *The Self-Awareness Superhighway*, discussing it with your coach, mentor or line manager, listening to some podcasts or watching some TED Talks. Write down what you want to do next to help you develop your listening skills.

You could also seek feedback from others to find out if they score your behaviour the same, similar or different. *The Self-Awareness Superhighway* will tell you more about the Self-Awareness Compass Quiz, which offers you a way to ask others for constructive feedback to help you on your leadership journey.

Your Reflections Journal

Choose a score for all nine points on the Self-Awareness Compass

9 is the most positive score, 1 is the most negative and 5 is the neutral point.

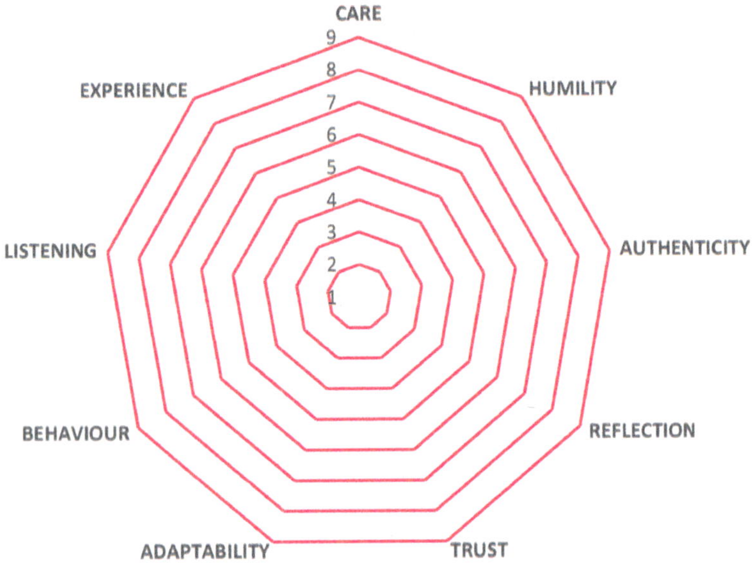

Thinking about the three layers of self-aware leadership – reflection, recognition and regulation – write down…

- your reflection on your hard and relational skills
- your impact on others
- what changes you want to make to your behaviour to do things differently next time.

Choose a score for all nine points on the Self-Awareness Compass

9 is the most positive score, 1 is the most negative and 5 is the neutral point.

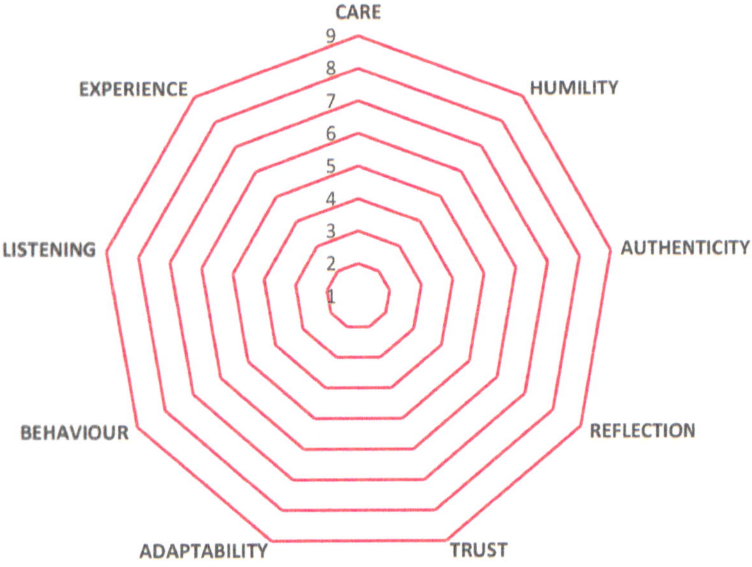

Thinking about the three layers of self-aware leadership – reflection, recognition and regulation – write down…

- your reflection on your hard and relational skills
- your impact on others
- what changes you want to make to your behaviour to do things differently next time.

Choose a score for all nine points on the Self-Awareness Compass

9 is the most positive score, 1 is the most negative and 5 is the neutral point.

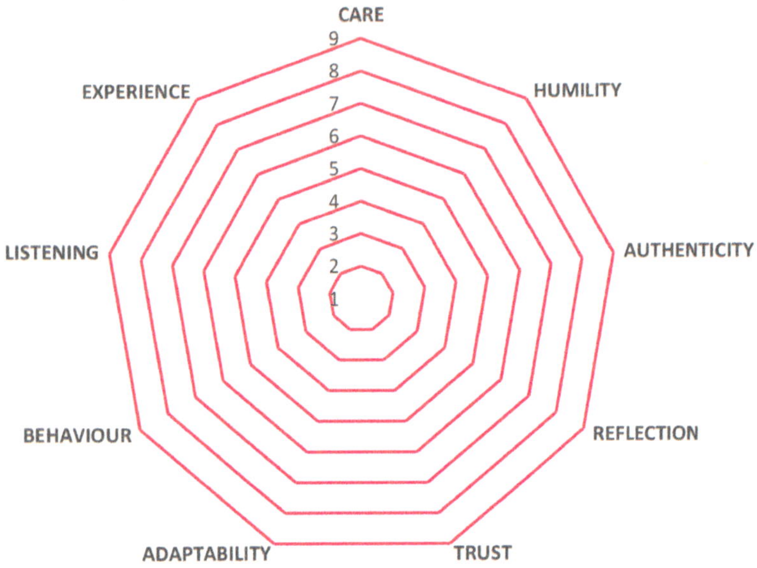

Thinking about the three layers of self-aware leadership – reflection, recognition and regulation – write down…

- your reflection on your hard and relational skills
- your impact on others
- what changes you want to make to your behaviour to do things differently next time.

Choose a score for all nine points on the Self-Awareness Compass

9 is the most positive score, 1 is the most negative and 5 is the neutral point.

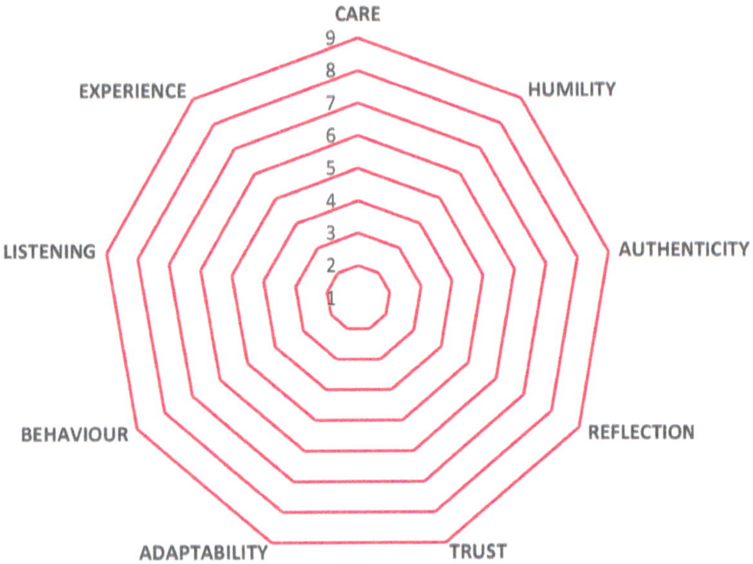

Thinking about the three layers of self-aware leadership – reflection, recognition and regulation – write down…

- your reflection on your hard and relational skills
- your impact on others
- what changes you want to make to your behaviour to do things differently next time.

Choose a score for all nine points on the Self-Awareness Compass

9 is the most positive score, 1 is the most negative and 5 is the neutral point.

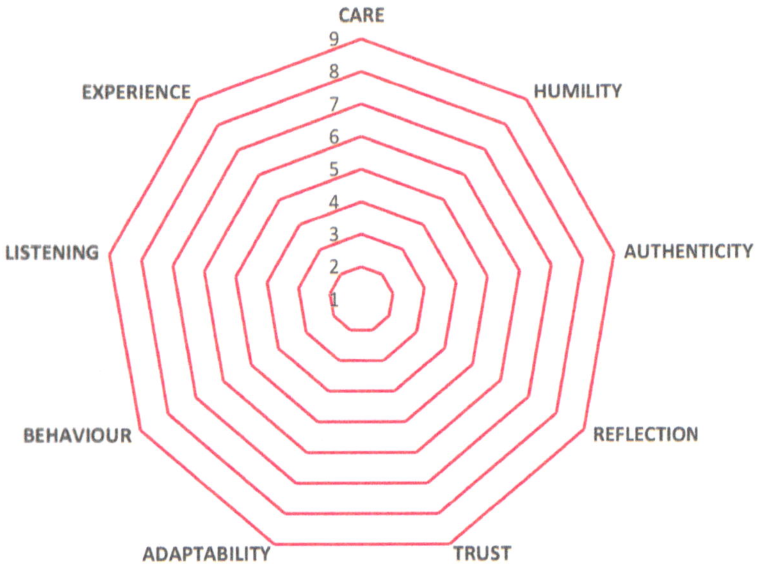

Thinking about the three layers of self-aware leadership – reflection, recognition and regulation – write down…

- your reflection on your hard and relational skills
- your impact on others
- what changes you want to make to your behaviour to do things differently next time.

Choose a score for all nine points on the Self-Awareness Compass

9 is the most positive score, 1 is the most negative and 5 is the neutral point.

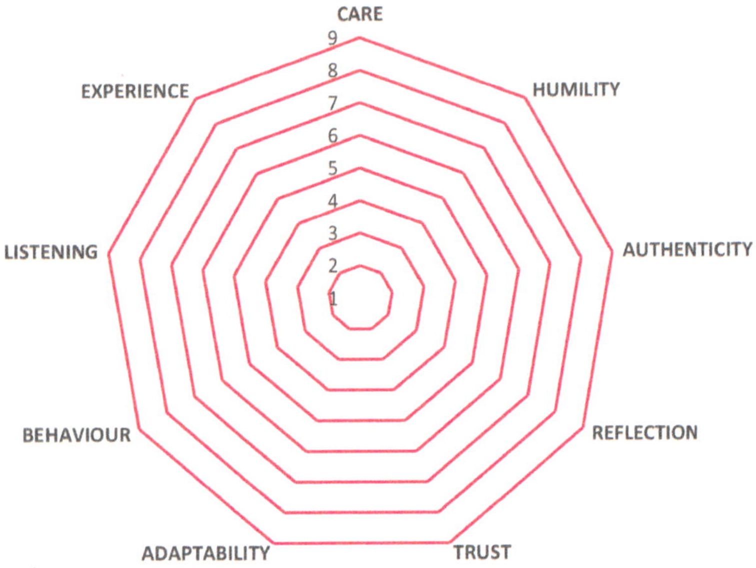

Thinking about the three layers of self-aware leadership – reflection, recognition and regulation – write down…

- your reflection on your hard and relational skills
- your impact on others
- what changes you want to make to your behaviour to do things differently next time.

Choose a score for all nine points on the Self-Awareness Compass

9 is the most positive score, 1 is the most negative and 5 is the neutral point.

Thinking about the three layers of self-aware leadership – reflection, recognition and regulation – write down…

- your reflection on your hard and relational skills
- your impact on others
- what changes you want to make to your behaviour to do things differently next time.

Choose a score for all nine points on the Self-Awareness Compass

9 is the most positive score, 1 is the most negative and 5 is the neutral point.

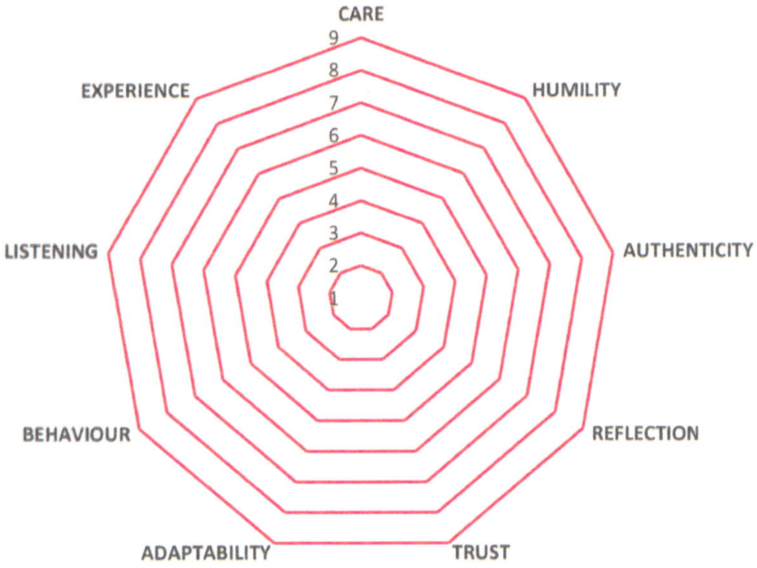

Thinking about the three layers of self-aware leadership – reflection, recognition and regulation – write down…

- your reflection on your hard and relational skills
- your impact on others
- what changes you want to make to your behaviour to do things differently next time.

Choose a score for all nine points on the Self-Awareness Compass

9 is the most positive score, 1 is the most negative and 5 is the neutral point.

Thinking about the three layers of self-aware leadership – reflection, recognition and regulation – write down…

- your reflection on your hard and relational skills
- your impact on others
- what changes you want to make to your behaviour to do things differently next time.

Choose a score for all nine points on the Self-Awareness Compass

9 is the most positive score, 1 is the most negative and 5 is the neutral point.

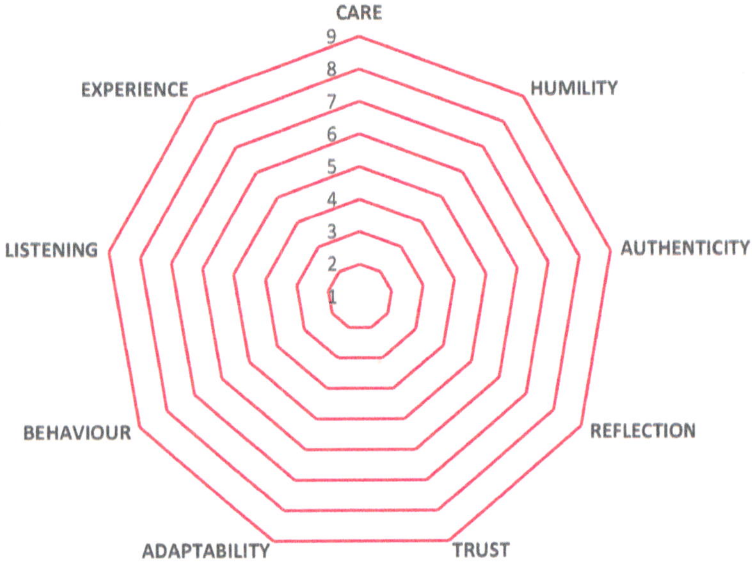

Thinking about the three layers of self-aware leadership – reflection, recognition and regulation – write down…

- your reflection on your hard and relational skills
- your impact on others
- what changes you want to make to your behaviour to do things differently next time.

Choose a score for all nine points on the Self-Awareness Compass

9 is the most positive score, 1 is the most negative and 5 is the neutral point.

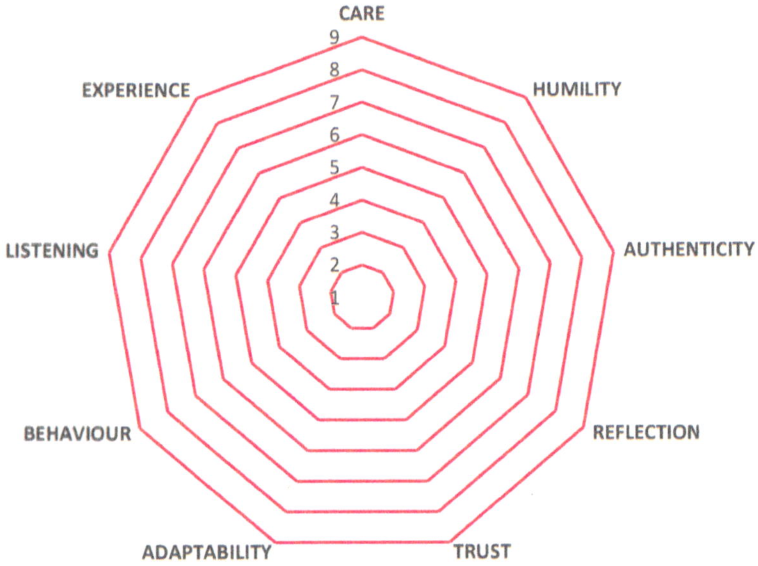

Thinking about the three layers of self-aware leadership – reflection, recognition and regulation – write down…

- your reflection on your hard and relational skills
- your impact on others
- what changes you want to make to your behaviour to do things differently next time.

Choose a score for all nine points on the Self-Awareness Compass

9 is the most positive score, 1 is the most negative and 5 is the neutral point.

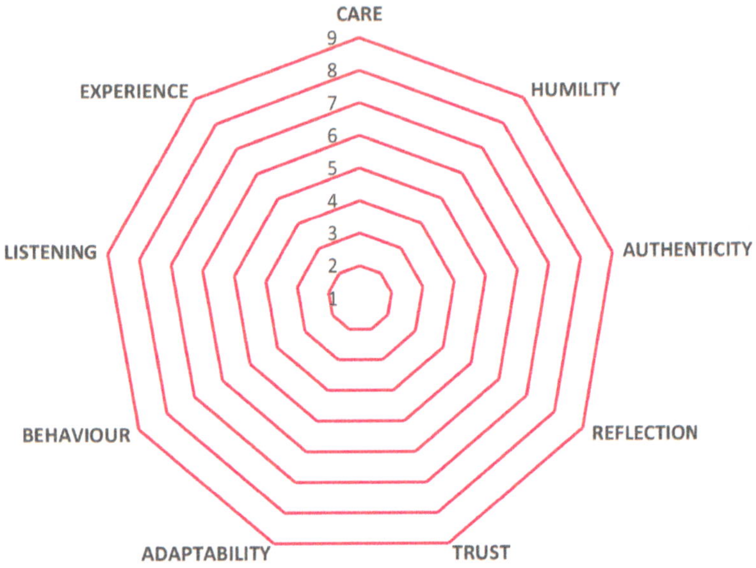

Thinking about the three layers of self-aware leadership – reflection, recognition and regulation – write down…

- your reflection on your hard and relational skills
- your impact on others
- what changes you want to make to your behaviour to do things differently next time.

Choose a score for all nine points on the Self-Awareness Compass

9 is the most positive score, 1 is the most negative and 5 is the neutral point.

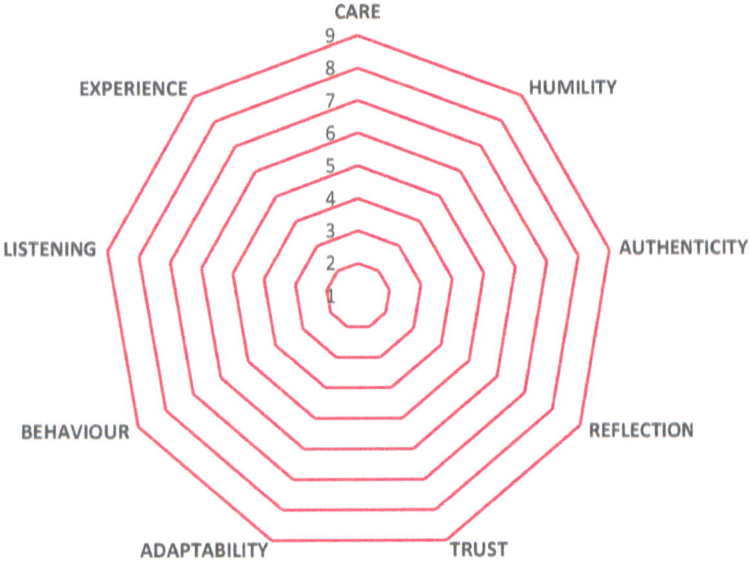

Thinking about the three layers of self-aware leadership – reflection, recognition and regulation – write down…

- your reflection on your hard and relational skills
- your impact on others
- what changes you want to make to your behaviour to do things differently next time.

Choose a score for all nine points on the Self-Awareness Compass

9 is the most positive score, 1 is the most negative and 5 is the neutral point.

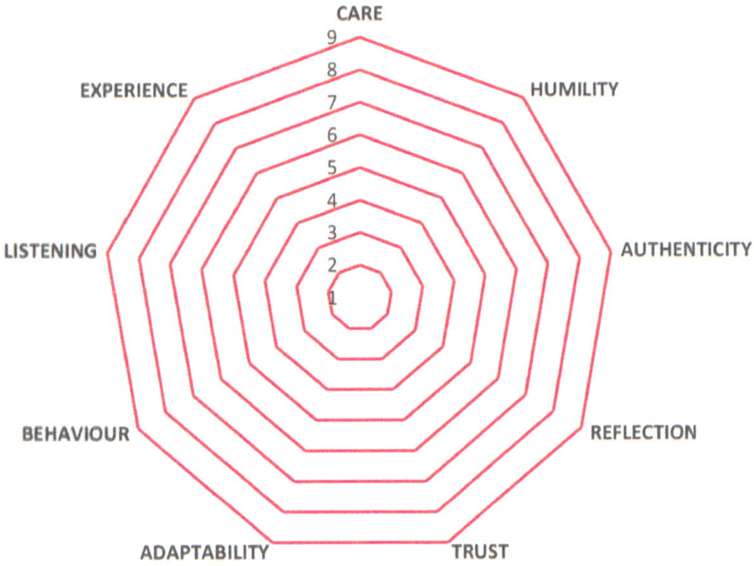

Thinking about the three layers of self-aware leadership – reflection, recognition and regulation – write down…

- your reflection on your hard and relational skills
- your impact on others
- what changes you want to make to your behaviour to do things differently next time.

Choose a score for all nine points on the Self-Awareness Compass

9 is the most positive score, 1 is the most negative and 5 is the neutral point.

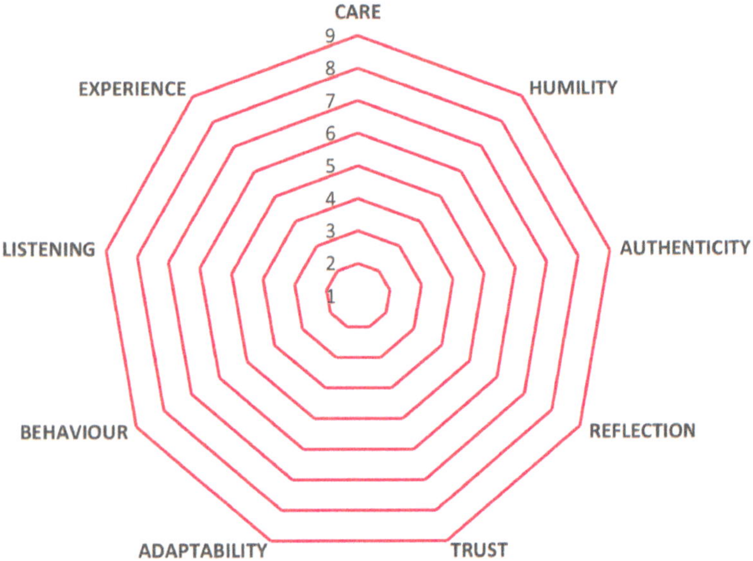

Thinking about the three layers of self-aware leadership – reflection, recognition and regulation – write down…

- your reflection on your hard and relational skills
- your impact on others
- what changes you want to make to your behaviour to do things differently next time.

Choose a score for all nine points on the Self-Awareness Compass

9 is the most positive score, 1 is the most negative and 5 is the neutral point.

Thinking about the three layers of self-aware leadership – reflection, recognition and regulation – write down…

- your reflection on your hard and relational skills
- your impact on others
- what changes you want to make to your behaviour to do things differently next time.

Choose a score for all nine points on the Self-Awareness Compass

9 is the most positive score, 1 is the most negative and 5 is the neutral point.

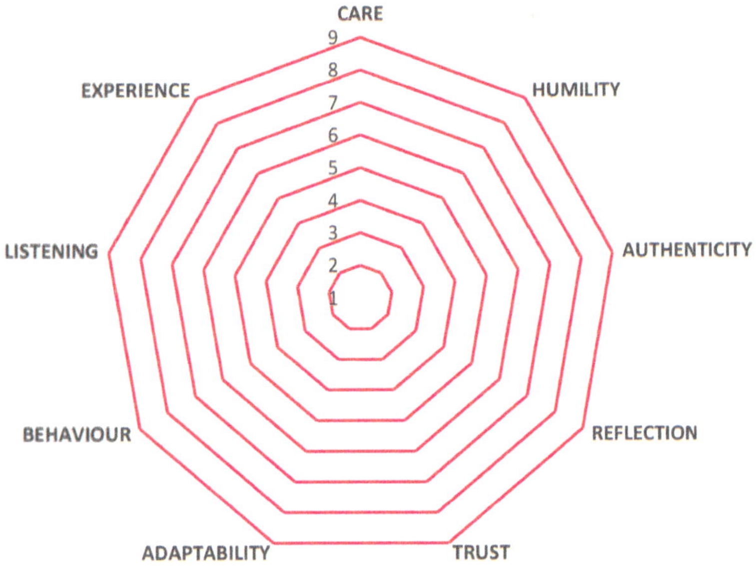

Thinking about the three layers of self-aware leadership – reflection, recognition and regulation – write down…

- your reflection on your hard and relational skills
- your impact on others
- what changes you want to make to your behaviour to do things differently next time.

Choose a score for all nine points on the Self-Awareness Compass

9 is the most positive score, 1 is the most negative and 5 is the neutral point.

Thinking about the three layers of self-aware leadership – reflection, recognition and regulation – write down…

- your reflection on your hard and relational skills
- your impact on others
- what changes you want to make to your behaviour to do things differently next time.

Choose a score for all nine points on the Self-Awareness Compass

9 is the most positive score, 1 is the most negative and 5 is the neutral point.

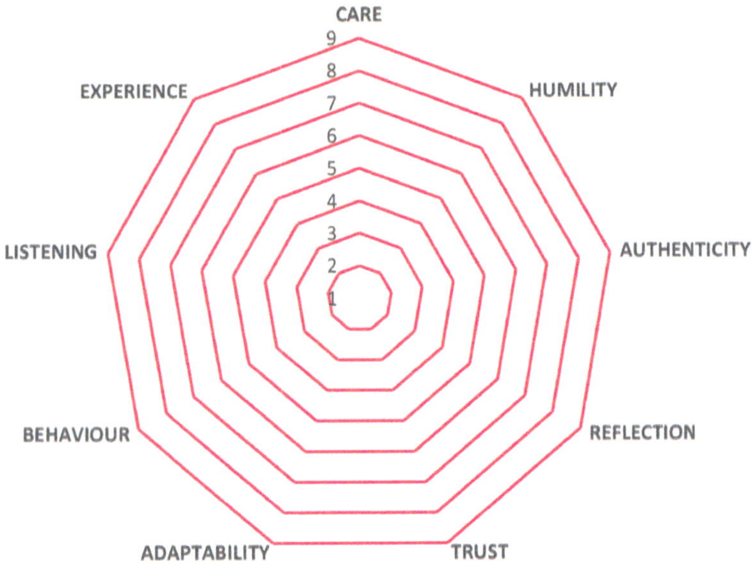

Thinking about the three layers of self-aware leadership – reflection, recognition and regulation – write down…

- your reflection on your hard and relational skills
- your impact on others
- what changes you want to make to your behaviour to do things differently next time.

Choose a score for all nine points on the Self-Awareness Compass

9 is the most positive score, 1 is the most negative and 5 is the neutral point.

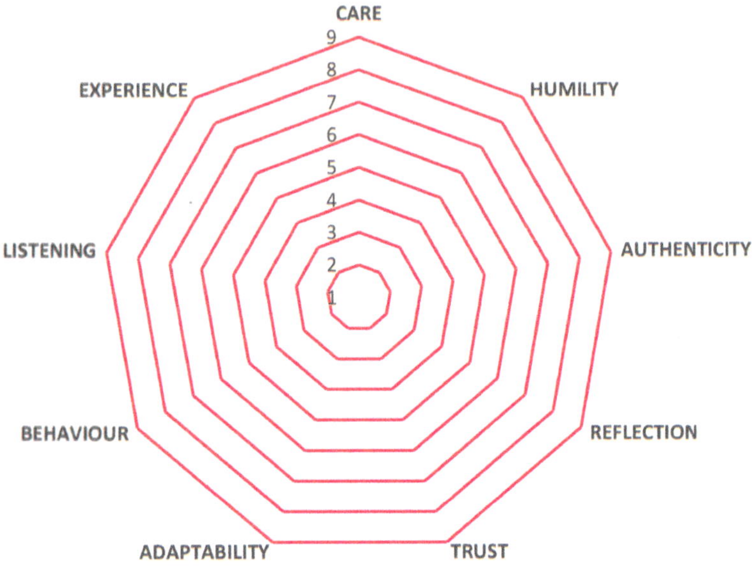

Thinking about the three layers of self-aware leadership – reflection, recognition and regulation – write down…

- your reflection on your hard and relational skills
- your impact on others
- what changes you want to make to your behaviour to do things differently next time.

Choose a score for all nine points on the Self-Awareness Compass

9 is the most positive score, 1 is the most negative and 5 is the neutral point.

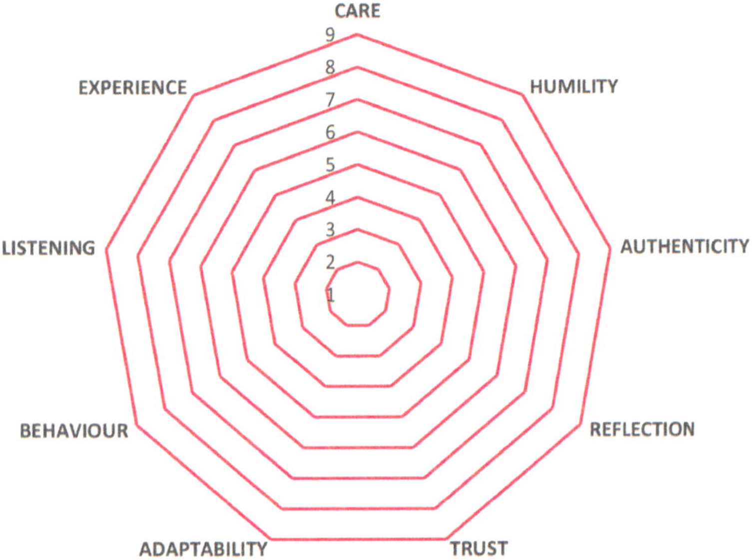

Thinking about the three layers of self-aware leadership – reflection, recognition and regulation – write down…

- your reflection on your hard and relational skills
- your impact on others
- what changes you want to make to your behaviour to do things differently next time.

Choose a score for all nine points on the Self-Awareness Compass

9 is the most positive score, 1 is the most negative and 5 is the neutral point.

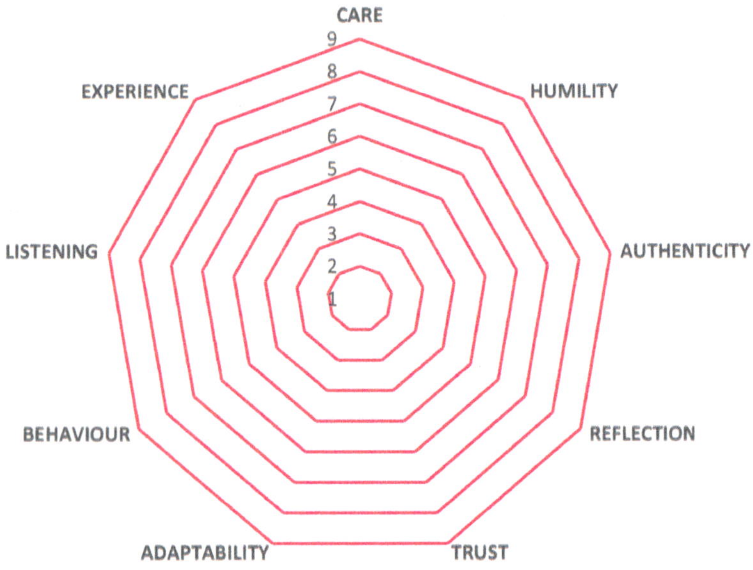

Thinking about the three layers of self-aware leadership – reflection, recognition and regulation – write down…

- your reflection on your hard and relational skills
- your impact on others
- what changes you want to make to your behaviour to do things differently next time.

Choose a score for all nine points on the Self-Awareness Compass

9 is the most positive score, 1 is the most negative and 5 is the neutral point.

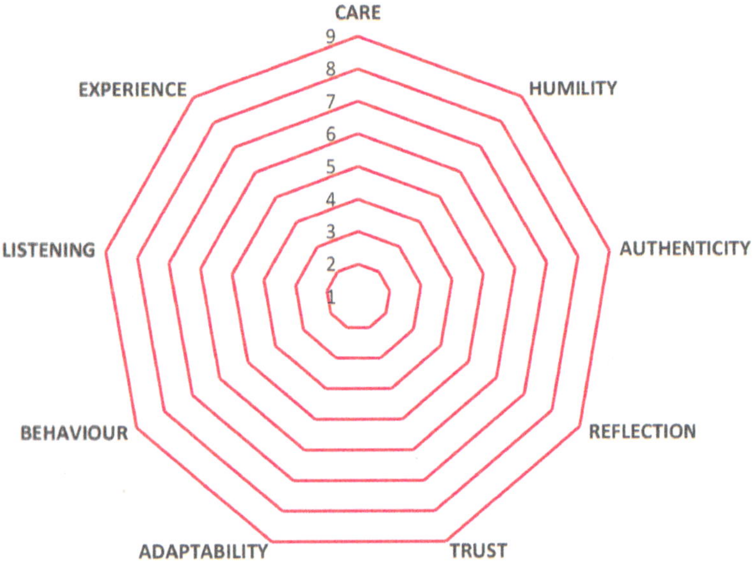

Thinking about the three layers of self-aware leadership – reflection, recognition and regulation – write down…

- your reflection on your hard and relational skills
- your impact on others
- what changes you want to make to your behaviour to do things differently next time.

Choose a score for all nine points on the Self-Awareness Compass

9 is the most positive score, 1 is the most negative and 5 is the neutral point.

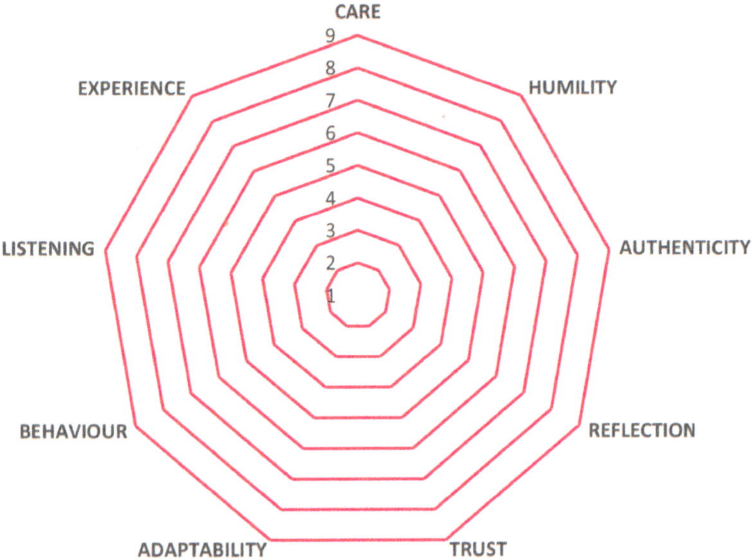

Thinking about the three layers of self-aware leadership – reflection, recognition and regulation – write down…

- your reflection on your hard and relational skills
- your impact on others
- what changes you want to make to your behaviour to do things differently next time.

Choose a score for all nine points on the Self-Awareness Compass

9 is the most positive score, 1 is the most negative and 5 is the neutral point.

Thinking about the three layers of self-aware leadership – reflection, recognition and regulation – write down…

- your reflection on your hard and relational skills
- your impact on others
- what changes you want to make to your behaviour to do things differently next time.

Choose a score for all nine points on the Self-Awareness Compass

9 is the most positive score, 1 is the most negative and 5 is the neutral point.

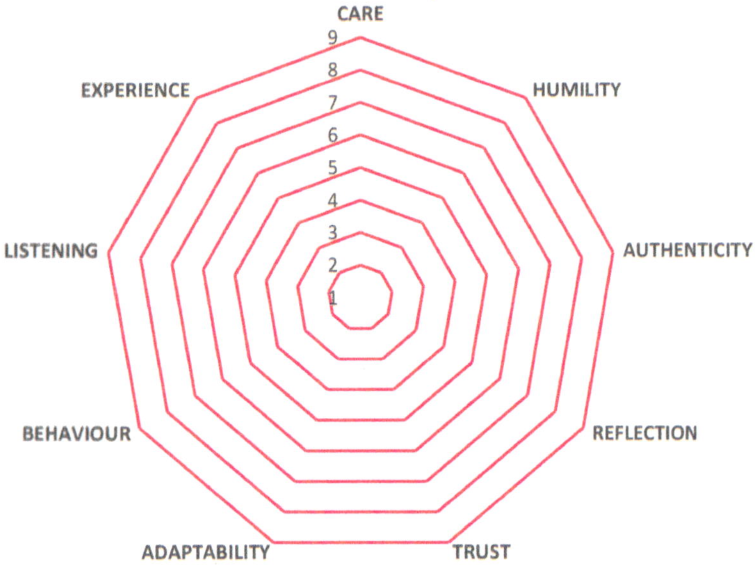

Thinking about the three layers of self-aware leadership – reflection, recognition and regulation – write down…

- your reflection on your hard and relational skills
- your impact on others
- what changes you want to make to your behaviour to do things differently next time.

Choose a score for all nine points on the Self-Awareness Compass

9 is the most positive score, 1 is the most negative and 5 is the neutral point.

Thinking about the three layers of self-aware leadership – reflection, recognition and regulation – write down…

- your reflection on your hard and relational skills
- your impact on others
- what changes you want to make to your behaviour to do things differently next time.

Choose a score for all nine points on the Self-Awareness Compass

9 is the most positive score, 1 is the most negative and 5 is the neutral point.

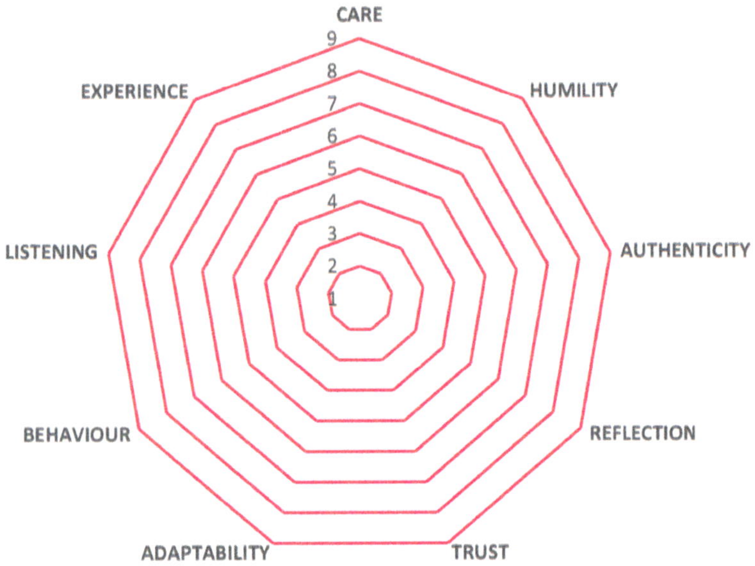

Thinking about the three layers of self-aware leadership – reflection, recognition and regulation – write down…

- your reflection on your hard and relational skills
- your impact on others
- what changes you want to make to your behaviour to do things differently next time.

Choose a score for all nine points on the Self-Awareness Compass

9 is the most positive score, 1 is the most negative and 5 is the neutral point.

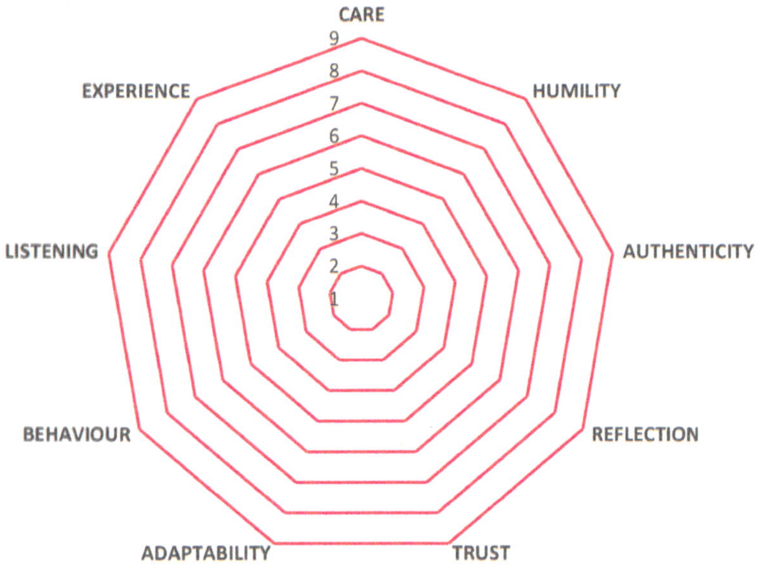

Thinking about the three layers of self-aware leadership – reflection, recognition and regulation – write down…

- your reflection on your hard and relational skills
- your impact on others
- what changes you want to make to your behaviour to do things differently next time.

Choose a score for all nine points on the Self-Awareness Compass

9 is the most positive score, 1 is the most negative and 5 is the neutral point.

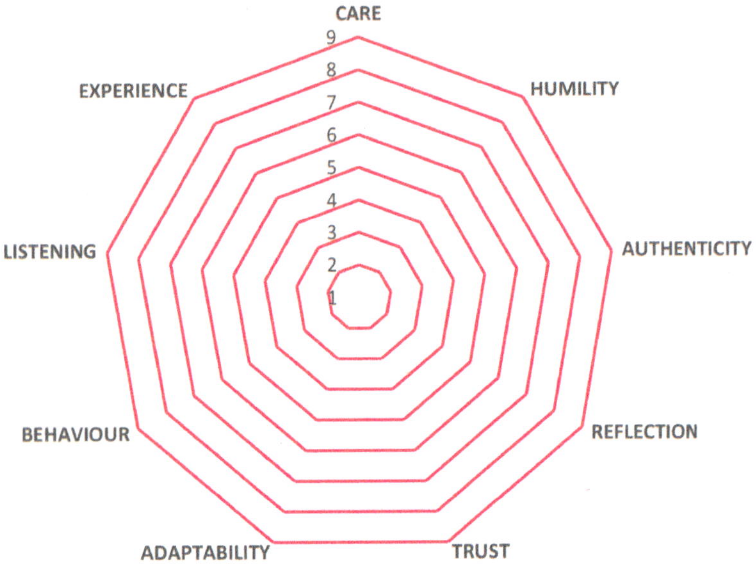

Thinking about the three layers of self-aware leadership – reflection, recognition and regulation – write down…

- your reflection on your hard and relational skills
- your impact on others
- what changes you want to make to your behaviour to do things differently next time.

Choose a score for all nine points on the Self-Awareness Compass

9 is the most positive score, 1 is the most negative and 5 is the neutral point.

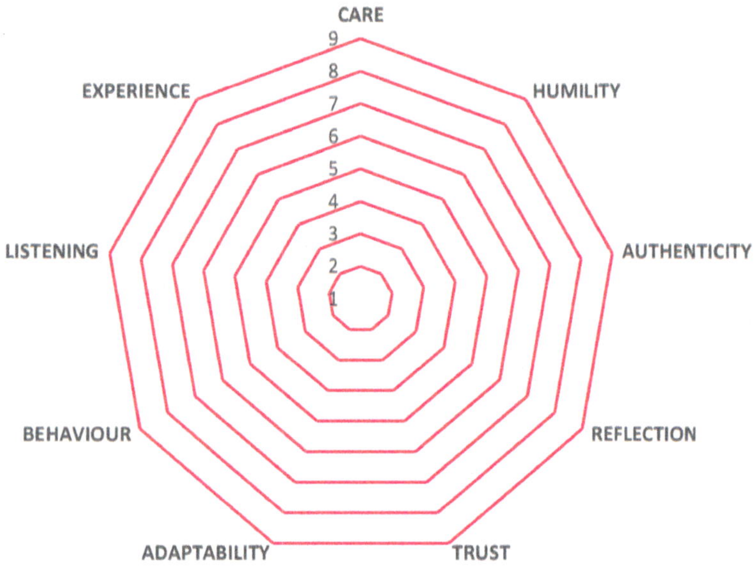

Thinking about the three layers of self-aware leadership – reflection, recognition and regulation – write down…

- your reflection on your hard and relational skills
- your impact on others
- what changes you want to make to your behaviour to do things differently next time.

Choose a score for all nine points on the Self-Awareness Compass

9 is the most positive score, 1 is the most negative and 5 is the neutral point.

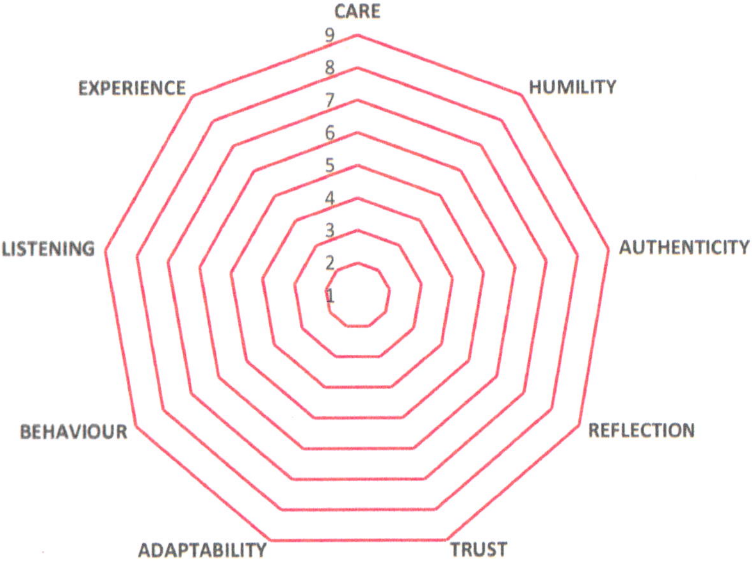

Thinking about the three layers of self-aware leadership – reflection, recognition and regulation – write down…

- your reflection on your hard and relational skills
- your impact on others
- what changes you want to make to your behaviour to do things differently next time.

Choose a score for all nine points on the Self-Awareness Compass

9 is the most positive score, 1 is the most negative and 5 is the neutral point.

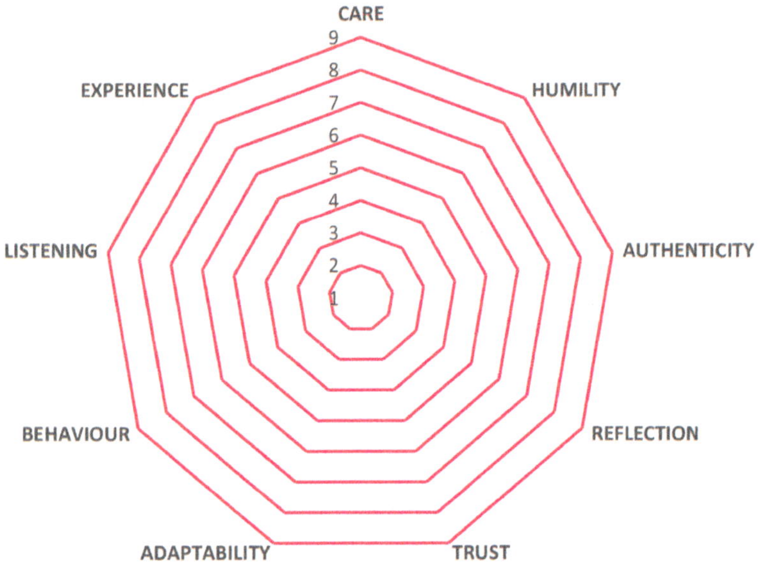

Thinking about the three layers of self-aware leadership – reflection, recognition and regulation – write down…

- your reflection on your hard and relational skills
- your impact on others
- what changes you want to make to your behaviour to do things differently next time.

Choose a score for all nine points on the Self-Awareness Compass

9 is the most positive score, 1 is the most negative and 5 is the neutral point.

Thinking about the three layers of self-aware leadership – reflection, recognition and regulation – write down…

- your reflection on your hard and relational skills
- your impact on others
- what changes you want to make to your behaviour to do things differently next time.

Choose a score for all nine points on the Self-Awareness Compass

9 is the most positive score, 1 is the most negative and 5 is the neutral point.

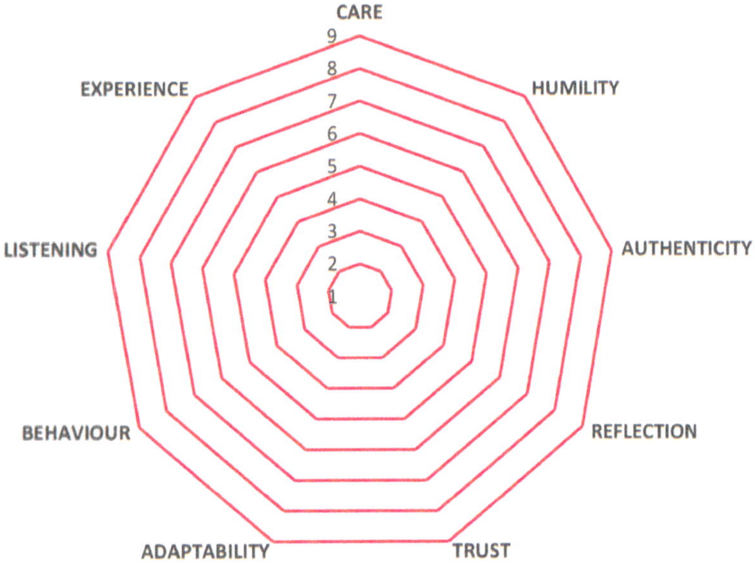

Thinking about the three layers of self-aware leadership – reflection, recognition and regulation – write down…

- your reflection on your hard and relational skills
- your impact on others
- what changes you want to make to your behaviour to do things differently next time.

Choose a score for all nine points on the Self-Awareness Compass

9 is the most positive score, 1 is the most negative and 5 is the neutral point.

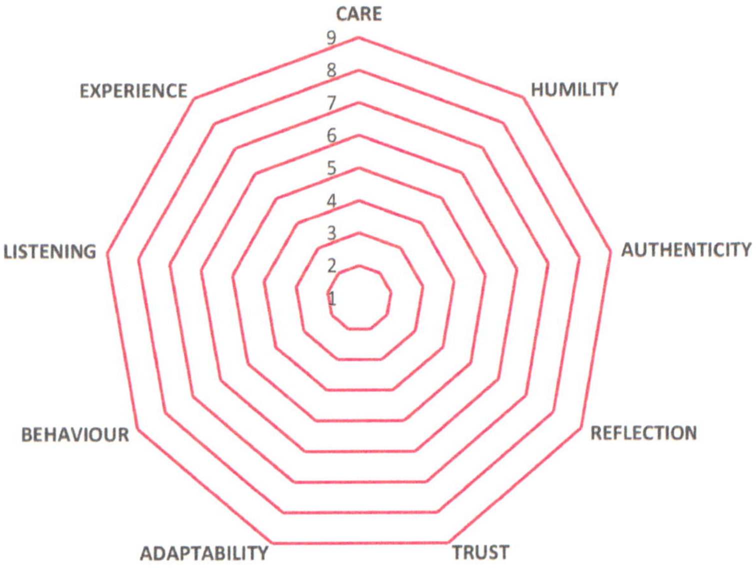

Thinking about the three layers of self-aware leadership – reflection, recognition and regulation – write down…

- your reflection on your hard and relational skills
- your impact on others
- what changes you want to make to your behaviour to do things differently next time.

Choose a score for all nine points on the Self-Awareness Compass

9 is the most positive score, 1 is the most negative and 5 is the neutral point.

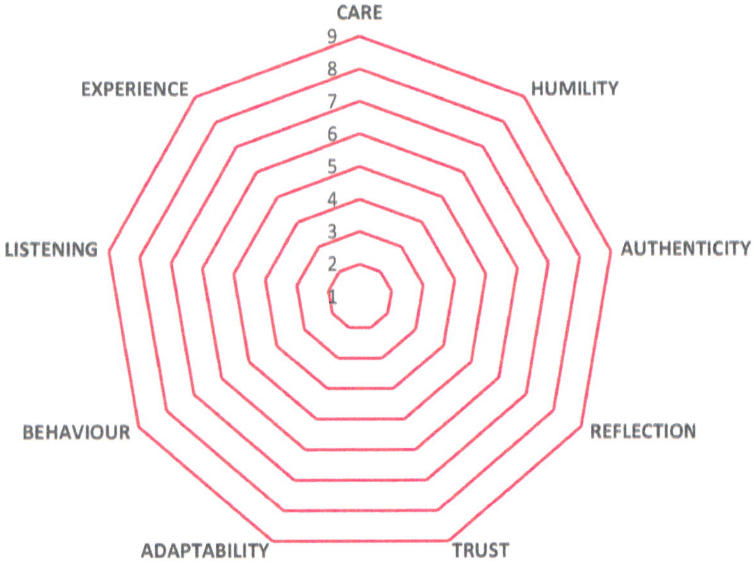

Thinking about the three layers of self-aware leadership – reflection, recognition and regulation – write down…

- your reflection on your hard and relational skills
- your impact on others
- what changes you want to make to your behaviour to do things differently next time.

Choose a score for all nine points on the Self-Awareness Compass

9 is the most positive score, 1 is the most negative and 5 is the neutral point.

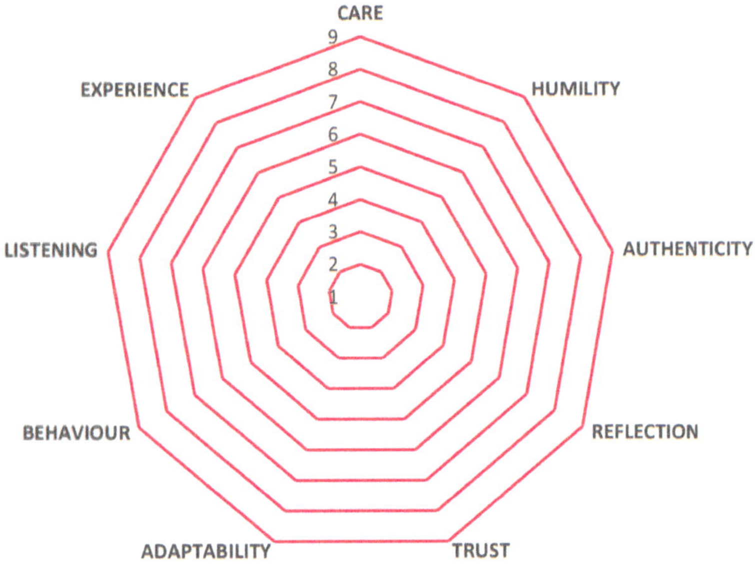

Thinking about the three layers of self-aware leadership – reflection, recognition and regulation – write down…

- your reflection on your hard and relational skills
- your impact on others
- what changes you want to make to your behaviour to do things differently next time.

Choose a score for all nine points on the Self-Awareness Compass

9 is the most positive score, 1 is the most negative and 5 is the neutral point.

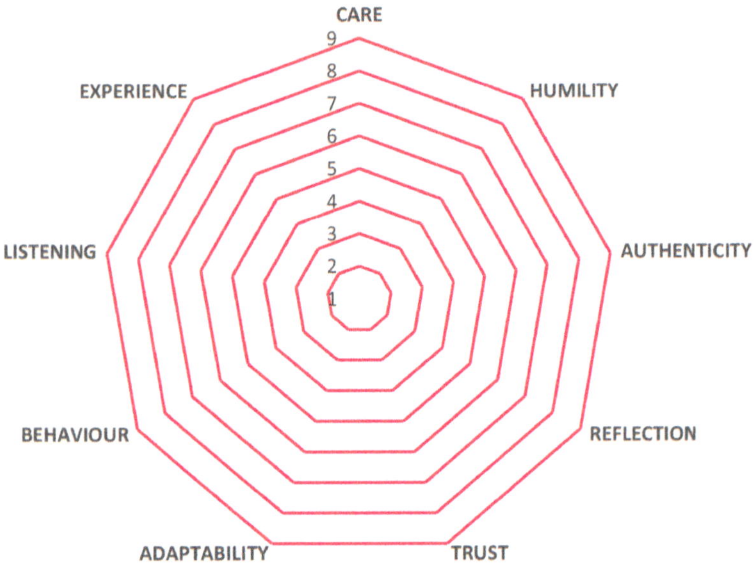

Thinking about the three layers of self-aware leadership – reflection, recognition and regulation – write down…

- your reflection on your hard and relational skills
- your impact on others
- what changes you want to make to your behaviour to do things differently next time.

Choose a score for all nine points on the Self-Awareness Compass

9 is the most positive score, 1 is the most negative and 5 is the neutral point.

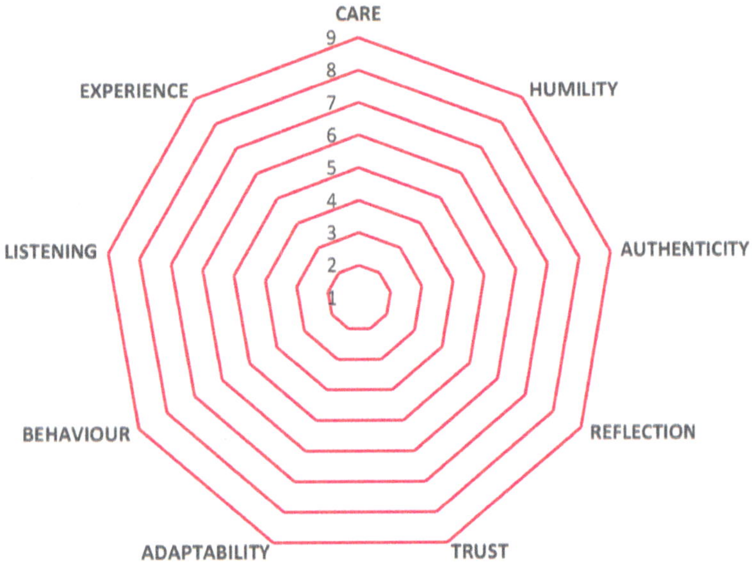

Thinking about the three layers of self-aware leadership – reflection, recognition and regulation – write down…

- your reflection on your hard and relational skills
- your impact on others
- what changes you want to make to your behaviour to do things differently next time.

Choose a score for all nine points on the Self-Awareness Compass

9 is the most positive score, 1 is the most negative and 5 is the neutral point.

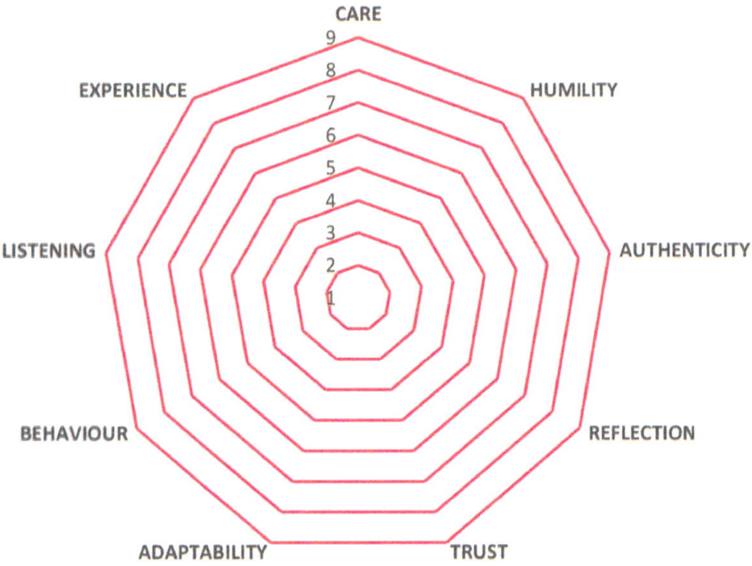

Thinking about the three layers of self-aware leadership – reflection, recognition and regulation – write down…

- your reflection on your hard and relational skills
- your impact on others
- what changes you want to make to your behaviour to do things differently next time.

Choose a score for all nine points on the Self-Awareness Compass

9 is the most positive score, 1 is the most negative and 5 is the neutral point.

Thinking about the three layers of self-aware leadership – reflection, recognition and regulation – write down…

- your reflection on your hard and relational skills
- your impact on others
- what changes you want to make to your behaviour to do things differently next time.

Choose a score for all nine points on the Self-Awareness Compass

9 is the most positive score, 1 is the most negative and 5 is the neutral point.

Thinking about the three layers of self-aware leadership – reflection, recognition and regulation – write down…

- your reflection on your hard and relational skills
- your impact on others
- what changes you want to make to your behaviour to do things differently next time.

Choose a score for all nine points on the Self-Awareness Compass

9 is the most positive score, 1 is the most negative and 5 is the neutral point.

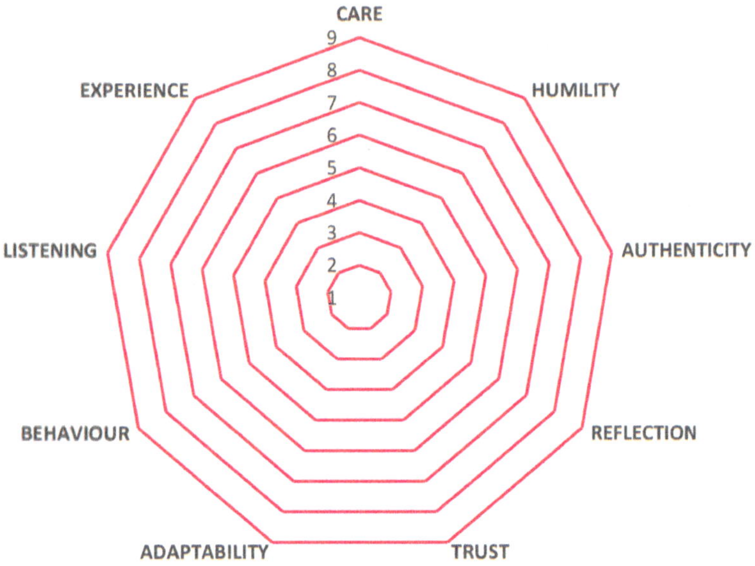

Thinking about the three layers of self-aware leadership – reflection, recognition and regulation – write down…

- your reflection on your hard and relational skills
- your impact on others
- what changes you want to make to your behaviour to do things differently next time.

Choose a score for all nine points on the Self-Awareness Compass

9 is the most positive score, 1 is the most negative and 5 is the neutral point.

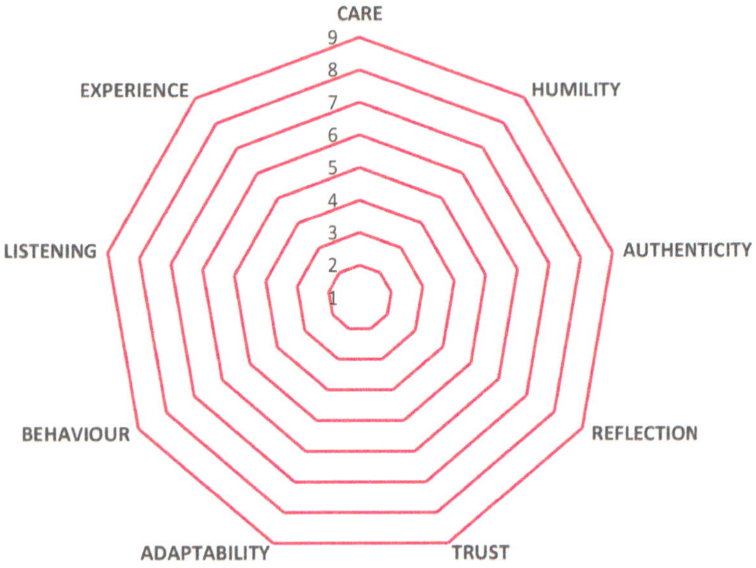

Thinking about the three layers of self-aware leadership – reflection, recognition and regulation – write down…

- your reflection on your hard and relational skills
- your impact on others
- what changes you want to make to your behaviour to do things differently next time.

Choose a score for all nine points on the Self-Awareness Compass

9 is the most positive score, 1 is the most negative and 5 is the neutral point.

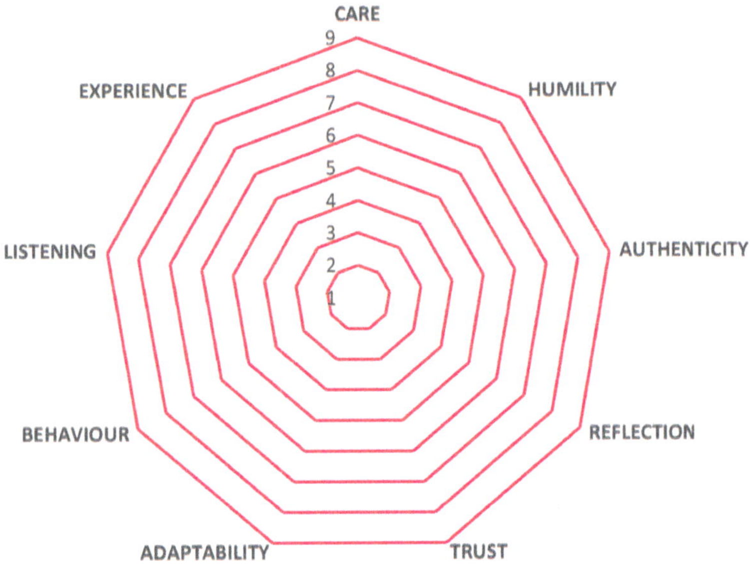

Thinking about the three layers of self-aware leadership – reflection, recognition and regulation – write down…

- your reflection on your hard and relational skills
- your impact on others
- what changes you want to make to your behaviour to do things differently next time.

Choose a score for all nine points on the Self-Awareness Compass

9 is the most positive score, 1 is the most negative and 5 is the neutral point.

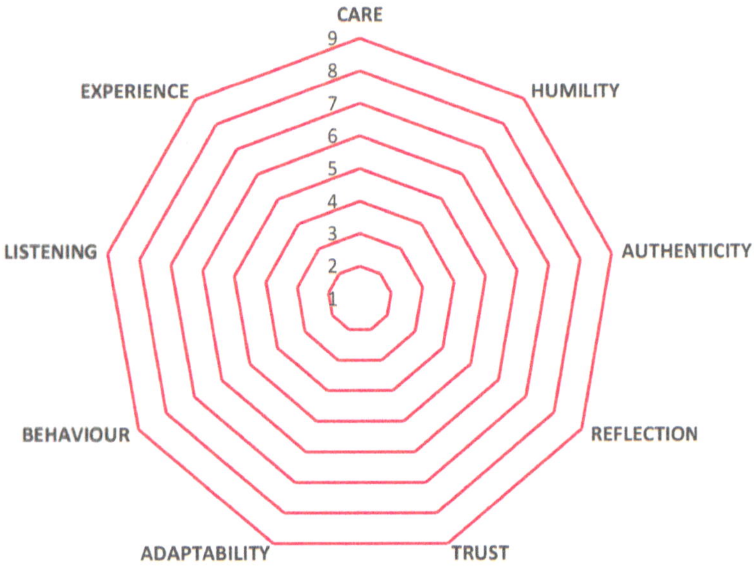

Thinking about the three layers of self-aware leadership – reflection, recognition and regulation – write down…

- your reflection on your hard and relational skills
- your impact on others
- what changes you want to make to your behaviour to do things differently next time.

Choose a score for all nine points on the Self-Awareness Compass

9 is the most positive score, 1 is the most negative and 5 is the neutral point.

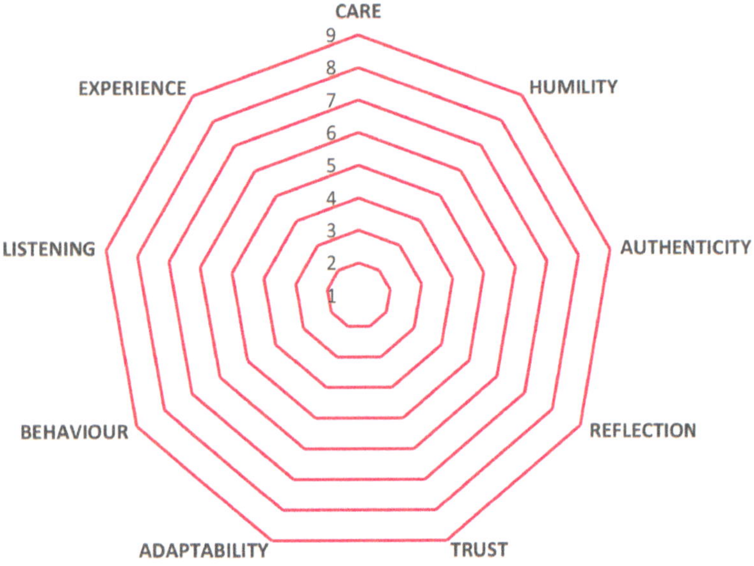

Thinking about the three layers of self-aware leadership – reflection, recognition and regulation – write down…

- your reflection on your hard and relational skills
- your impact on others
- what changes you want to make to your behaviour to do things differently next time.

Choose a score for all nine points on the Self-Awareness Compass

9 is the most positive score, 1 is the most negative and 5 is the neutral point.

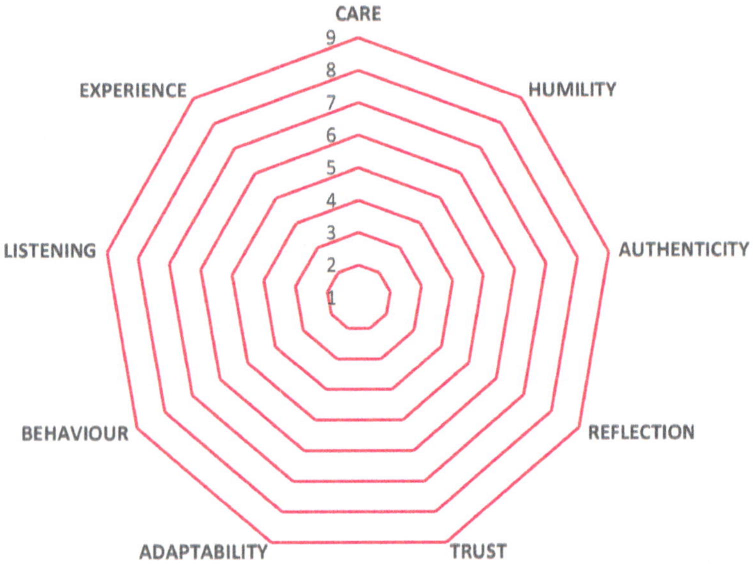

Thinking about the three layers of self-aware leadership – reflection, recognition and regulation – write down…

- your reflection on your hard and relational skills
- your impact on others
- what changes you want to make to your behaviour to do things differently next time.

Choose a score for all nine points on the Self-Awareness Compass

9 is the most positive score, 1 is the most negative and 5 is the neutral point.

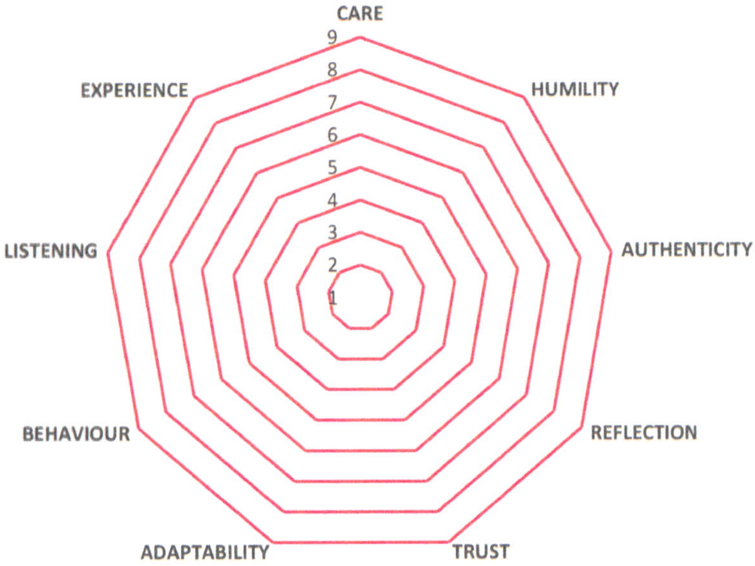

Thinking about the three layers of self-aware leadership – reflection, recognition and regulation – write down…

- your reflection on your hard and relational skills
- your impact on others
- what changes you want to make to your behaviour to do things differently next time.

Choose a score for all nine points on the Self-Awareness Compass

9 is the most positive score, 1 is the most negative and 5 is the neutral point.

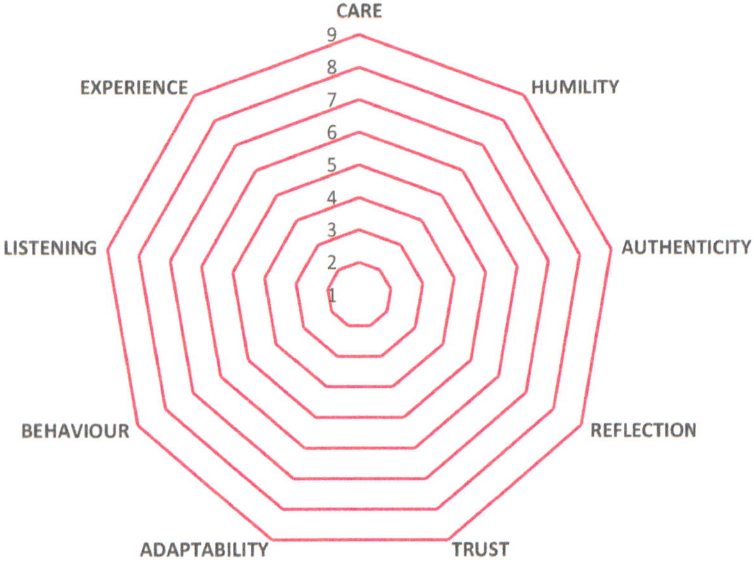

Thinking about the three layers of self-aware leadership – reflection, recognition and regulation – write down…

- your reflection on your hard and relational skills
- your impact on others
- what changes you want to make to your behaviour to do things differently next time.

Choose a score for all nine points on the Self-Awareness Compass

9 is the most positive score, 1 is the most negative and 5 is the neutral point.

Thinking about the three layers of self-aware leadership – reflection, recognition and regulation – write down…

- your reflection on your hard and relational skills
- your impact on others
- what changes you want to make to your behaviour to do things differently next time.

The Back Pages

Resources for You

- ***The Self-Awareness Superhighway: Charting Your Leadership Journey***

- **Knowing Self Knowing Others Website**
  www.ksko.co.uk

Blog: Access all of my blog posts via my website.

Social Media: My website will take you to all of my social media accounts on LinkedIn, Instagram, Facebook, YouTube, TikTok, Substack, etc. You can also click on the link to my Linktree, which brings all my links together in one place.

Newsletter: You can sign up for my weekly podcast top takeaways newsletter and monthly reflections newsletter.

- ***The Knowing Self Knowing Others Podcast***

Audio: You can listen to the podcast on Apple Podcasts, Spotify, Amazon Music, Goodpods, Podchaser, Deezer, Listen Notes and more. By visiting my website and clicking on 'podcast' and 'listen', you can access it straight from your browser too.

Video: Many of my podcasts are now also available in video, along with audio on YouTube, which you can access via the little icons on the top right of my website.

Clips: Short video clips of top takeaways from podcast episodes can be found on TikTok and Instagram.

Praise for
The Self-Awareness Superhighway

"Dr Nia Thomas offers a compelling and insightful guide for leaders seeking to enhance their effectiveness by understanding the impact of their behaviour and actions. Dr Thomas provides a raw and honest perspective, encouraging leaders to step outside themselves and critically reflect on their leadership capabilities, gaps and potential. This book is a must read for leaders aspiring to deepen their self-awareness and enhance their impact, whether they be an experienced manager or new to their leadership journey. Dr Nia Thomas's blend of research-backed guidance and personal anecdotes creates a compelling narrative that will resonate with leaders striving to create positive change within their organisation."

T. Poore
Charitable-Sector CEO, Public-Sector Experienced

"A seemingly effortless journey through self-awareness that encourages the traveller to stop at the junctions of theory, practice, paradox and dilemma, destined in growing their leadership."

E. Piera
Leadership Development Specialist, Coach and Lecturer

"What sets this book apart is its foundation in extensive research and Dr Thomas's personal experiences, which enrich the content with authenticity and relatability. By weaving together theory and practical insights, the author creates a compelling narrative that resonates with leaders navigating their own leadership journeys."

"It is truly a treasure trove of knowledge and I'm so impressed at how you have assimilated your personal research, that of others and podcast guest insights, along with examples of lived experience, to provide a hugely valuable, credible and engaging resource!"

"You have a real skill at taking academic research and concepts and communicating them in a way that is clear and accessible."

"Dr Thomas emphasizes the importance of introspection and self-awareness in creating environments that prioritise empathy, diversity and inclusivity."

About the Author

Dr Nia D. Thomas is an expert leader who talks the talk and walks the walk. She is an academically awarded researcher in self-aware leadership and practises self-aware leadership every single day in her role as a director of a children's charity.

Before moving to the charitable sector, Nia spent over 20 years working across the public sector in local government, the National Health Service and Civil Service, predominantly in Wales and, in the last few years, England.

Throughout her career, Nia has been interested in working relationships: the dynamics between people and the impact both good and bad relationships have on individuals, their wellbeing and ability to do their work. This led her to develop an interest in self-awareness, leader effectiveness and leadership at all levels, which became the focus of her doctoral research.

Nia was born and bred in St David's, the UK's smallest city, before moving to Cardiff for university. She spent a year in Japan during her undergraduate days and settled in Cardiff after graduation. She later moved north to the South Wales Valleys, where she remained and made it her home. She met her husband through their shared love of cars, which is a passion they still enjoy. Together, they moved to London before the pandemic to pursue career opportunities.

Nia now lives in west Essex, within easy reach of London, where she loves to visit coffee shops and is on a mission to find the perfect gluten-free cake and the fanciest, tastiest ice-cream – preferably both together!

You can find Nia at www.ksko.co.uk.

You can contact Nia at info@ksko.co.uk.

Printed in Great Britain
by Amazon

50494000R00076